Life BREEZE

Live Your Dream & Serve Your Purpose

LILLIAN WORTH

WESTBOW
PRESS

A DIVISION OF THOMAS NELSON
& ZONDERVAN

Scripture taken from the King James Version of the Bible.

WestBow Press books may be ordered through booksellers or by contacting:

WestBow Press
A Division of Thomas Nelson & Zondervan
1663 Liberty Drive
Bloomington, IN 47403
www.westbowpress.com
1 (866) 928-1240

ISBN: 978-1-4908-7367-1 (sc)
ISBN: 978-1-4908-7368-8 (hc)
ISBN: 978-1-4908-7366-4 (e)

Library of Congress Control Number: 2015904152

Print information available on the last page.

WestBow Press rev. date: 04/22/2015

CONTENTS

DEDICATION

These poems were written for
the searching, lost, and broken-hearted children of God. You are beautiful
and special to your almighty Creator. May you live in the knowledge of
God's plan and purpose for your life, and may your light always shine.

They are dedicated to
my husband. Your love and support are an ongoing source
of strength, encouragement, and guidance in my life,

and to
my three precious children. You are an inspiration, and I am
forever grateful for the love and joy you bring to our lives.

PREFACE

This book is more than a collection of poems; it is a journey of self-discovery. These poems and insights were written to help bring you to the knowledge of how wonderful and worthy you truly are, to guide you in your search for happiness, and to discover the plan God has for your life. Through prayer and reflection as you read these poems, the Holy Spirit will reveal to you the promises awaiting you and that you were created for a divine destiny and purpose.

I would encourage you to say the *Insight Prayer* before reading each poem. The *Reflections* page is there for you to journal all you feel, see, and hear as the Holy Spirit reveals God's message for you. Information on how to create a Vision Board and personal Mission Statement can be found on my website:

www.lillianworth.com

If you choose, each poem can be read as a weekly reflection with revelation through journaling. I would suggest that the poem be read a few times and meditated upon to allow the Holy Spirit to speak to you. At the end of this journey, may you be secure in the knowledge of God's immeasurable love for you. Everything is okay! God has your back and an amazing plan for your life.

[Words shown in italics are when God, Jesus, or the Holy Spirit is speaking.]

INTRODUCTION

Almost fifteen years had passed since our first child, a beautiful baby girl, was born. Life in the suburbs for this average middle-class family was good. One month later our world was turned upside down when our daughter ran away from home. This was to be the first in a series of runaways, and at sixteen years of age she left home and was living on the streets.

What had happened? As Christians we had believed we were safe from extreme and destructive adolescent behavior. Our children all attended private Christian schools, went to church on Sundays, and belonged to youth groups. This made no sense. The impact on our family was devastating. Her two younger siblings were confused, hurt, and angered by her rejection; her father and I were distraught with concern for her safety.

We could not stop our daughter's life from spiraling out of control in a haze of drug abuse and petty street crimes to support her addicted lifestyle. During this dark and turbulent time in my life, the Lord fully opened my eyes to the pain and brokenness that impact so many of us in our privileged society. A whole generation is being robbed of its potential and identity through the spiritual attack of an Enemy whose sole purpose is to steal, kill, and destroy. Too many of our children are being sucked up into a vacuum of hopelessness and despair, losing their way and sight of the promises awaiting them from a loving and abundant God.

There were many times when Facebook was the only means I had of knowing that my daughter was alive. I checked daily for updates to see if she had posted anything on a friend's or her wall. While reading these Facebook pages I saw memes, song lyrics, and poems conveying messages of rebellion, anger, hopelessness, and despair. It was everywhere. Teenagers were absorbing this negativity and darkness on a daily basis, and sadly, many were relating to it.

I recall with clarity a post that I read depicting so much pain and hopelessness. It showed a life given over to drugs from which there was no return—a life sold out for the temporary narcotic charms of an illicit substance. In anguish I called out to God, not only for my child, but for every lost and hurting soul out there. Whatever their circumstances, whether it be drugs, self-harming, bullying, low self-esteem, rejection, loneliness, or confusion, *Lord, please, there must be something to combat this. Please give me something,* was my cry. At that moment my heart broke for every lost, hurting, and tormented child of God. My loving and merciful heavenly Father heard my plea and gave me an answer through poetry.

Two days later I felt compelled to pick up a pen and write. Never before had I written poetry, yet suddenly the words began to flow. These poems were not written as a cathartic expression of the pain our family endured but were a download from the Holy Spirit to bring comfort to those going through difficult times and trauma. Within two weeks I had penned forty poems. I had no idea where each poem would take me as I began to write. One thing I knew for sure was that the poems were divinely inspired, and writing them has been one of the most humbling experiences of my life. These poems were written for the healing, guidance, and restoration of the hurt and lost.

Today, three years after a spiritual attack that led my daughter into the wilderness, into a dark world of drugs and despair, she has returned home. Thankfully, throughout her experience she remembered her identity in Christ, her birthright as a precious child of God. She held on to the outstretched hand of her forgiving and merciful heavenly Father. He helps her to rebuild the pieces of her life and lovingly restores her to wholeness. Sadly, too many do not know their identity; they struggle and face the evil forces in our world lost and alone. For them my hope is that they will come to know their ever-present and merciful God, his unending love and forgiveness, and will accept Jesus as their Lord and Savior. In Jesus there is hope, healing, and restoration.

INSIGHT

As I read these words today,
Help me, Lord, to hear
All it is you want to say
As you draw me near.

Show me what I need to see;
Open up my eyes.
Let these words speak to me.
Help me to be wise.

Guide me in all I do
In my life today.
Create in me a heart anew.
Lord, this is what I pray.

REFLECTIONS

(What God's Spirit Said to Me)

WHO AM I?

A beautiful baby,
A wonderful child,
A questioning teenager—
Some confusion inside.

The choices are many,
The answers not clear.
The way can seem hazy,
And sometimes there's fear.

Will they all like me?
Am I part of the crowd?
Do I belong?
I could yell it out loud.

But deep down inside me
I hear a gentle voice say,
You're my child, my loved one;
I'll show you the way.

I am here with you always;
I never will leave.
I live here within you;
I'm the air that you breathe.

I will strengthen and guide you;
I'll comfort and love.
Just trust me; I'm with you.
I was sent from above.

REFLECTIONS

(What God's Spirit Said to Me)

THE ANSWER

The questions are many;
The answer's just one.
But how do I find it?
I don't know where to run.

Whom do I ask?
What should I say?
Will I look stupid?
Will they send me away?

It's driving me crazy;
Where do I turn?
How can I find it?
When will I learn?

The mistakes I make over,
The things that I do,
The problems I cause
Are more than a few.

But here in my heart
The answer abides.
I'm always here with you;
In you I reside.

Mistakes we all make
And problems we cause.
But we are all human;
That's part of our flaws.

I made you to love me;
And in you, I live.
I'm always here with you,
And I always forgive.

REFLECTIONS

(What God's Spirit Said to Me)

HOLD ON

I hurt,
I cry.
The pain—
Oh, why?

It's all too hard;
It hurts too much.
I ache inside;
I want to give up.

To end it all
Would be so easy:
To stop the pain
That never leaves me.

Then in my heart
I hear a quiet voice say,
I'm here with you;
We'll find the way.

Hold on to me;
I'm always here.
I'll be your strength
And make the way clear.

I promise you this:
I won't let you go.
I'm all that you need.
I love you more than you know.

So keep up hope
When the going gets rough.
Hold on to me;
I'm more than enough.

REFLECTIONS

(What God's Spirit Said to Me)

THE MISSION

The harvest is plenty,
But workers are few.
The mission's astounding;
We're all part of the crew.

The world, it needs us;
It's full of pain and despair.
Our message is hopeful;
It's always been there.

The years have not changed it;
It's always the same:
*I love you; I'm with you.
In you I remain.*

*I came here to save you,
To bless you as well,
To love you and keep you
When in me you dwell.*

*I'm always here with you;
This you do know.
But many are lost,
And to these you will go.*

*Tell them the good news,
For to me they belong.
We're all in this together;
Together we're strong.*

*The enemy comes to harm us,
But it is to no avail.
Because I'm always here with you
His efforts will all fail.*

*So always stay with me;
Be strong and be bold.
And tell them the good news—
That I paid for their souls.*

REFLECTIONS

(What God's Spirit Said to Me)

HOLY TEMPLE

My body is special,
Made by him.
It is a holy temple;
He resides within.

God gave it to me,
But it's also his home.
I'm never to harm it;
My heart is his throne.

So to trash it with junk,
Sex, drugs, and the like
Is a sin before heaven.
My body's filled with his light.

I choose to be healthy
And always say no
To everything evil
That will block off God's flow.

Heavenly gifts
Descend from above,
Like love, peace, and joy,
And someone to love.

Reflections

(What God's Spirit Said to Me)

A Sea of Faces

I look around me, and what do I see?
Millions of faces looking at me.
Eyes staring out blankly in heavenly droves;
Their future is aimless, with nowhere to go.

They've lost their way in a very large crowd
And forgotten about me; I'm never allowed
To enter their thoughts and their minds, you see,
Because they've filled it with nonsense that wasn't from me.

Seduced by the world, they've shut me out
And forgotten what life is really about.
The peace I could bring them, the happiness, too,
Are here for the taking, but they have no clue.

To know me and love me is more precious than gold,
More precious than diamonds; I can never be sold.
I live deep within them, and I want them to turn
To their Rock, their cornerstone, and be willing to learn.

If they gave their lives back over to me
They would know what it feels like to truly be free.
Their lives would be filled with heavenly love
And my peace that comes from up above.

REFLECTIONS

(What God's Spirit Said to Me)

DRUGS

Drugs are a weapon
The Enemy will use
To get you to lie,
Steal, cheat, and abuse.

Your life, it was given
By God up above
To be blessed in this world
And filled with his love.

But Satan, he comes
To steal, kill, and destroy.
If you're wise, you won't let him;
Don't fall for his ploy.

Drugs are a trick
The Enemy will use.
At first they feel good,
But they give you the blues.

Drugs tear at your heart,
Your mind, and your soul.
You'll wish you'd not tried them;
You'll lose all control.

Drugs are a tool
The Enemy will use.
But you're not a fool;
Don't fall for his ruse.

REFLECTIONS

(What God's Spirit Said to Me)

OPPOSITES

The world is full of opposites;
That's the way that it was made.
The earth, the stars, the land, and sea
Are foundations that God laid.

It was all part of God's perfect plan;
He knew it from the start.
He spoke it into being,
And he lives within your heart.

There's hot, there's cold, there's good and bad.
There's up, there's down, and more.
But the most important thing is
That we all should know the score.

He created you for someone
Who's special, just for you.
He created you to love him
And love that person, too.

Sometimes there comes confusion
About whom that person is,
But just be still and wait on God;
The timing is all his.

There's boy, there's girl, the two attract;
That's the way that it was done.
And when it's all in God's time,
The two turn into one.

God always had his perfect plan;
He knew you from the start.
He knew who'd truly love you,
And who would steal your heart.

REFLECTIONS

(What God's Spirit Said to Me)

ATTITUDE

Attitude is everything;
Don't let it bring you down.
It's the way you live your life;
It is a glorious crown.

Inside us lives a Spirit
That is powerful and true.
It guides us through our daily lives
And helps us when we're blue.

It strengthens and upholds us
And always shows the way.
Just listen to it closely
And you will hear it say:

I live here within you;
I'm here to make you strong.
If you listen to my voice
You never will go wrong.

I've been sent here to guide you
And help you on your way.
And you will surely win
When you follow what I say.

I came down from God above;
I'm full of grace and truth.
I'll bring you joy and happiness
And eternal youth.

Because you are my own dear child
I'll always keep you strong.
I live here within you,
And to me you belong.

For all who invite me in
They, too, can know
What it's like to be my child
As I help them grow.

REFLECTIONS

(What God's Spirit Said to Me)

AFRAID

He knows how it feels to be afraid
And know not what to do.
He, too, experienced this;
It was God who got him through.

Get down on your knees and pray;
The answer will always come—
What it is you need to do
And how it will be done.

You have his Holy Spirit;
He'll help to get you through.
He wouldn't have let this happen
If it were something you couldn't do.

The experience will strengthen you;
It will change your life, you know.
With him you will make it through,
And there'll be many seeds to sow.

You see, the Enemy always comes
To try to bring you down.
But face your fear and beat him,
And you'll wear a victor's crown.

We have a mighty Savior
Who is powerful and strong.
He makes a way before us,
Even when it seems so long.

Because we are more than conquerors
We've been sent out to all to say:
In Jesus there is victory,
And Jesus is the way.

REFLECTIONS

(What God's Spirit Said to Me)

MISTY FEAR

Fear is but a foggy mist;
It cannot hold you back.
Just use the light within you;
It's a spiritual attack.

Fear is an illusion;
When you take it on you'll see
That when you look it in the face,
It will have to flee.

Never let it stop you;
Just send it on its way.
Speak the truth against it,
And then it cannot stay.

It does not belong with you
And cannot hold you back.
Use your spiritual arsenal
To fight a spiritual attack.

You'll see the fear dissipate,
Then you can push on through
To what it is you want to change
And what you were called to do.

REFLECTIONS

(What God's Spirit Said to Me)

LIFE BREEZE

Don't be concerned
With everyday things.
Try not to worry,
Or stress it will bring.

There is an approach
That is always easy,
A flow to your life
That makes life breezy.

Trust in God
In all that you do
To go before you
And see you through.

Stop and listen to the birds,
See the flowers,
Catch the breeze,
And you will go through life with ease.

REFLECTIONS

(What God's Spirit Said to Me)

THE MAD SAD

If you're feeling bullied,
Then you must surely know
That bullies need to prove a point,
But you can help them grow.

You see that really bullying
Is fear turned inside-out.
Bullies are secretly frightened
By what you're all about.

There's something missing in their lives
That makes them very sad.
But they don't want the world to see it,
And so it makes them mad.

If only they could face it
For what it really is,
Bullies could find peace of mind
And true happiness.

So don't let bullies get you down;
The problem is not you.
It is the fear inside them
That someone might see through.

They're really in a lot of pain;
They need help to get it out.
So don't ever judge them
Or what they're all about.

Just be the face of Jesus,
His voice and his hands, too.
And always remember
That the problem is not you.

REFLECTIONS

(What God's Spirit Said to Me)

HEAD SPACE

Get out of your head
And in to your heart.
Let not the worries of this world
Tear you apart.

I'm here with you always;
My ways are all clear.
They only need you
To step out with no fear.

So don't stop and dwell on things;
Just trust me and go.
What waits ahead of you
I already know.

You have a destiny
That you'll one day live—
A divine appointment,
And there you will give.

The path is laid out for you.
Trust me; you'll see
What I shall do for you
And who you will be.

Then when it's done
And you turn and look back,
You'll know I was with you;
You were never in lack.

All that you needed
Was already there
Laid out before you.
You just had to care.

It was all about others,
Not only for you.
It's what you were made for
And what you will do.

REFLECTIONS

(What God's Spirit Said to Me)

Storms of Life

The breeze has turned into a storm;
There's tempest everywhere.
My life is so uncertain;
This has caught me unaware.

I thought that if I followed you,
It was good times all ahead.
How could this have happened?
Was I so misled?

A life of ease and comfort,
Plain sailing all the way.
This is unexpected;
My life's in disarray.

When people now look at me,
How can I testify
To your faithfulness and glory—
How you always get me by?

But then I remember
About Jesus in the boat.
As the storm raged around them,
They all managed to stay afloat.

I guess that life is like that;
Storms happen on the way.
But think about who's in your boat,
And then, just stop and pray.

The storm, it always passes,
And a rainbow will appear.
Then you know God's smiling down,
Saying, *I told you I was near.*

REFLECTIONS

(What God's Spirit Said to Me)

Ask, Seek, Knock

There's a verse that comes to mind,
Written just for the blind.
No, not the blind by sight,
But for those without the light.

When life brings you down
And you can only frown,
All that you need to do
Is follow this simple clue.

If you have no strength, yourself,
Look to God and ask for help.
Give your cares to him and pray,
Help will be on its way.

Seek the Lord in all you do;
He will help you make it through.
Trust him with your every care;
He's always with you, everywhere.

In your heart there is a door
That you had closed up before.
He's been knocking, but
you didn't know
How to let your problems go.

As you turn to him and say,
"Please take my cares away,"
The door to your heart
will open wide,
And he will come inside.

Now in your heart he'll
always dwell.
And even when all is not well,
Trust that he is always there
To help with your every care.

You will have peace of mind
That once had been so hard to find.
Whatever may come your way,
With him, you'll always be okay.

REFLECTIONS

(What God's Spirit Said to Me)

You're the One

God has a plan for your life
Without angst and without strife.
Follow his direction and see
What it is you were created to be.

The plan he has for you is good.
He always knew that he would
Use you in a particular way
So that he can have his say.

You see, he wants to tell us all:
Every one of us has a call.
He gave us gifts that we should use
To tell the others his good news.

We are all set apart
Right back from the very start.
He knew exactly what he would do;
He just needs us to see it through.

So gladly give your life to him.
His plan is best; you're born to win.
God knows precisely what is to be done.
He's chosen you; you're the one.

REFLECTIONS

(What God's Spirit Said to Me)

HOLY PRESENTS

I step into your holy presence.
What do I find?
All the promises that you've given
For this life of mine.

You come to me bearing gifts
Laid out for all to see.
I only need to trust in you
And all you do for me.

Your gift of love means everything;
I know the price you paid.
You gave your life up for me
So that I could be saved.

Your peace, it always covers me
And brings hope to every day.
I trust in you to always be
My light along the way.

Joy, it now fills my life;
Your presence is ever near.
With you always by my side
I never have to fear.

Your gifts are so precious to me.
The promises you've given
Bring love, hope, peace, and joy
From your life arisen.

REFLECTIONS

(What God's Spirit Said to Me)

FREE TO BE ME

It's time to be free,
Time to be me,
To take back control
And not lose my soul.

To realize your hold
Is only a lie.
I have the real truth
Deep down inside.

A power is in me—
A spirit so strong
That will overcome anything
That ever goes wrong.

When I tap into that life force
Then I will know:
You won't control me.
I just have to say no!

REFLECTIONS

(What God's Spirit Said to Me)

Whoa, Bro!

Whoa, bro; yeah, ya know?
Ya got the answers, dude.
Ya don't need anyone tellin' ya,
And ya always rude.

Hey, bro, you act so cool
When the world can see you.
But down inside there's
too much pain
To let anyone near you.

Your talk is tough; you got swag
Out there in the open.
But in the quiet with no one there,
You are really broken.

There is a hurt, and it goes deep;
It just won't let you go.
And so you keep a lid on it;
You never let it show.

Drugs, alcohol, sex, and weed
Have been the things you use
To try to help dull the pain.
But now you just abuse.

Your world is dark; all
hope seems gone.
You don't know what to do.
But reach down deep inside you,
And let your spirit through.

There is a strength within you,
And it's nobody's fool.
Just take each day as it comes;
That's the Golden Rule.

Don't worry about the future;
Forget about the past.
You only have the present;
For one day you can last.

Just take each day that's given—
You only have today—
And use the power within you.
It won't let you stray.

You'll have a new tomorrow
That's bright as it can be.
The past is done and over with,
And now you're truly free.

REFLECTIONS

(What God's Spirit Said to Me)

Are We There Yet?... Are We There Yet?
(The Potter's Hands)

Don't be in a hurry;
You just need to wait on him.
He's got his plan for your life,
And you'll surely win.

Even when the road gets rough
And problems come your way,
The plan is still right on track.
God's working with the clay.

You see, you're in the potter's hands;
He's molding you for the task
Of what lies ahead of you
And what he's going to ask.

The process can be painful;
It hurts as he pulls and rolls.
But he's shaping you
the way he wants;
The potter is in control.

He fires up the furnace;
The heat it really burns.
It hurts so much you want to scream,
But this is where you learn.

Always trust in our Lord;
You know that you'll get through.
And as the heat goes up a notch,
He's in the furnace, too.

You see, he had to mold you
And craft you all the way.
You now know why it hurt so much;
God was working with the clay.

Now that it's all over
And you're feeling quite bemused,
You know the potter was at work.
He's got someone he can use.

So don't be in a hurry;
Wait on him and see
What it is you are to do
And who you're called to be.

REFLECTIONS

(What God's Spirit Said to Me)

THE DREAM TEAM

God planted a seed
Deep in my soul,
Which he watered and nurtured
And watched it grow.

The seed to my dream
Was always deep down,
And as I grew older
My turn came around.

I'll follow my dream
And follow my heart.
God planted it in me
Right from the start.

So whatever obstacles
May come my way,
I know to keep going;
My life's a relay.

God passed me the baton
When he planted the seed.
So I run to the finish line;
I've got all that I need.

It's all here within me;
I just need to access
All that enables me
To create my success.

I know I can do it
Because it's planted in me.
So I keep running the race;
I know I'll succeed.

REFLECTIONS

(What God's Spirit Said to Me)

TOGETHER

When life gets me down
And I feel weak,
I hold on to you;
You're all that I seek.

As the darkness around me
Comes closing in,
I search for the light
I know is within.

The weaker I get,
The stronger I am.
I don't need to do it;
Only you can.

When I am weak,
Then you are strong.
Because you are in me,
In you I belong.

I am the branch
And you are the vine.
You are my real strength—
A power divine.

Together, a tree,
Strong and upright,
Bearing much fruit.
What a glorious sight.

REFLECTIONS

(What God's Spirit Said to Me)

Sleepless Nights

I cry,
I weep,
I hurt so much
I cannot sleep.

My chest is tight;
Why can't I breathe?
My life is being choked
Out of me.

Thoughts keep racing
In my head.
I find no sleep
Here in my bed.

I toss and turn;
I'm still awake.
Not much more of this
Can I take.

In a desperate voice
I call your name.
Please help me, Lord;
I can't bear the pain.

Your loving arms
Envelop me
With warmth and comfort—
What I need.

Now I am safe;
Don't ever leave.
Your peace—
It washes over me.

REFLECTIONS

(What God's Spirit Said to Me)

THE BUTTERFLY

You don't know me;
You think you do.
My face is a mask
None can see through.

I've built walls;
They're all around
To keep me safe.
You'll gain no ground.

Here in my cocoon
Is where I'll stay.
Where no one sees me,
I'll hide away.

But I am trapped;
I need to break free.
I've created a prison
Only for me.

It's lonely in here.
It's time to come out
And find out what life
Is really about.

Can I trust them?
I don't know.
But I want to be free,
So I'll give it a go.

Instead of a cocoon,
I'm now wrapped in wings.
I feel so happy
With all life brings.

I look in the mirror;
A butterfly I see.
To my surprise
The butterfly is me.

REFLECTIONS

(What God's Spirit Said to Me)

SANCTUARY

I am sad.
I feel weak.
I feel so low
I don't want to speak.

Just leave me alone
Here in my room.
I don't want company—
Just my gloom.

Don't talk to me;
I don't want to hear.
I won't be listening.
Do I make myself clear?

Your voice, it sounds
Like babble to me.
I want to be on my own,
Can't you see?

People I thought
That I could trust
Have let me down;
It hurts so much.

I need to think
And figure it out.
If you come in again,
I know I'll shout.

In my sadness
I ponder the Word
And start to feel better.
I know you've heard.

You're here with me
In my room,
Giving me comfort,
Dispelling the gloom.

REFLECTIONS

(What God's Spirit Said to Me)

BESTY

Everyone's talking,
But they don't include me.
I feel so lonely;
Can anyone see?

They all have friends,
But I have none.
I'm always alone—
Not part of the fun.

They don't seem to notice
As I pass by,
Or when I'm sitting and standing
Right by their side.

Nobody asks me,
"How was your day?
How are you doing?
Are you okay?"

I seem to be going
Through life all alone.
I don't have a best friend
To call my own.

But deep down inside me
I hear a gentle voice say,
*This is only a season;
It's not here to stay.*

*One day things will be different,
And you will have mates.
You'll be included;
You just have to wait.*

*Until then you're learning
To trust only me.
All through the years
I'm your one true Besty.*

REFLECTIONS

(What God's Spirit Said to Me)

CONFUSION

I worry about my future
And what it is that I should do.
While others have it figured out,
I really have no clue.

I seem to go through my life
Drifting from one day to the next.
Sometimes they all roll into one,
And some days are just train wrecks.

I know I should apply myself
And focus on my goal.
But that is where the problem lies,
And I don't tell a soul.

I don't know exactly what it is
That I've been called to do.
I need some help to find it
And clear direction, too.

But then I hear a soft voice say,
Take that first small step;
A step in faith is all you need,
And I will do the rest.

You may not be quite ready yet;
Your future you don't know.
But I know what you're called to be,
And I will help you grow.

So just get up and make a start
In anything you please.
I will help you along the way;
You can set your mind at ease.

When I know the time is right
And you are ready for the task,
You will know what you're to do,
And what it is I ask.

REFLECTIONS

(What God's Spirit Said to Me)

HOLE IN MY SOUL

There is a hole in my soul,
An emptiness inside.
Even though I smile and talk,
The hole just feels so wide.

This hole is deep within me
That nothing ever fills.
Sometimes I feel such loneliness
Against my very will.

I wish I knew just what it was
Missing inside of me,
So I could try and change it;
Then I would be free.

As I search deep within
I hear a small voice say,
It's me you've been looking for;
I can show the way.

You see that hole is where I lived
Before you shut me out—
A hole that only I can fill
And turn your life about.

Just ask me in; I'm waiting.
I've been knocking at the door.
When I live within your heart
There'll be no emptiness anymore.

REFLECTIONS

(What God's Spirit Said to Me)

LOVE IS, LOVE DOES

Love isn't something that you feel;
It's something that you do.
It's about the other person,
Not just about you.

Love puts the other person's needs
Way above your own,
And brings a life of happiness
That isn't lived alone.

Love isn't just a passing fling;
Over the years you'll watch it grow.
As it fills up every part of you,
With it, you'll overflow.

Love is patience at its best.
It allows you to forgive,
And it always offers kindness
So in harmony we live.

Love, it never will let go
But doesn't hold on to wrongs.
It gives others what they need
To help make them strong.

Love, it will conquer all;
It always overcomes.
When you just hold on to it
Your lives are lived as one.

Love creates a unity
That none can undermine,
Because true and everlasting love
Comes from God; it's divine.

Reflections

(What God's Spirit Said to Me)

LIVING IN CREATION

It's a beautiful world we live in;
God made it just for us.
Each day is such a blessing;
Don't be in a rush.

Savor every moment
That's been given just for you,
And live here in the present.
It's the only thing to do.

Look at your surroundings—
Beauty is everywhere.
Take it in and let it fill you.
Live your life aware.

Creation is a witness
To how mighty our Lord is.
He made it all in such detail;
He's an intellectual whiz.

He then created science
To testify how it was made.
But God keeps some of his secrets;
He doesn't give them all away.

Be thankful for creation,
It's beauty to behold.
Such an awesome miracle—
Let it fill your soul.

REFLECTIONS

(What God's Spirit Said to Me)

MY LIFE IN YOUR HANDS

I give my life to you, Lord;
Teach me all your ways.
Show me who I am to be;
Don't let me go astray.

I'll try to always give you
My very, very best,
Even in the hard times
When life puts me to the test.

Help me when I'm tempted
With all the worldly things.
Strengthen me to not give in,
For sorrow they will bring.

I only want to live my life
According to your plan.
Your plan is always best for me.
You are the great I Am!

REFLECTIONS

(What God's Spirit Said to Me)

FORGIVENESS

It's not easy to forgive, Lord,
The hurt done to me.
But in my soul I truly know
It's what will set me free.

To hold on to the bitterness
Will only cause despair
That won't easily release me.
I don't want to live life there.

I know that by forgiving
It's me who will be blessed.
Your favor is upon me
To help repair the mess.

Forgiveness is why you came
To take away our sin.
I know I can do it, too,
Because you live within.

As I am forgiven,
I, too, must forgive.
With you, it is possible;
In you, I will live.

Reflections

(What God's Spirit Said to Me)

FIERY AND HOT

Anger has a hold on you;
Don't let it explode.
You need to control it,
And let it go.

As a tirade of abuse
Flows freely from your lips,
Reach inside and stop it up.
It's coming from the pit.

Anger, fiery and hot,
The Enemy will use
To take away love, joy, and peace.
Don't let him get to you.

Just take a long, deep breath;
Feel the temperature go down.
You don't have to play his game;
No demon wins this round.

Now take another breath;
Make it long and sweet and slow.
Can you feel God's love and peace?
The anger's letting go.

Jesus is the Prince of Peace;
Feel his peace flowing through
Every fiber of your being.
Peace lives in you.

Give thanks for your savior,
His peace will set you free.
Anger has no place here;
You only have to breathe.

REFLECTIONS

(What God's Spirit Said to Me)

Ultimate Victory

Victory is mine.
The battle done,
The fight is over.
Jesus won!

I always look to the cross;
My battle was fought there.
Jesus has already claimed the prize,
And it's for me to share.

So even when the struggles come
And things in life go wrong,
I cast my eyes upon the cross.
It's there my cares belong.

Now two thousand
years have passed,
And the Enemy's just the same.
Still trying to wage his war,
His tactics never change.

The liar, he tries to confuse me
And divert my eyes from the cross.
He thinks if he can bring me down,
I'll believe my battle's lost.

But I always hold on to hope
And the battle Jesus fought.
Jesus holds the victory,
And my eternity, he bought.

So I live life to the fullest;
Victory is always mine.
No matter what may happen,
I always will be fine.

When I keep my eyes upon Jesus
And follow all his ways,
I have the ultimate victory.
My Savior rose from the grave.

REFLECTIONS

(What God's Spirit Said to Me)

OUT OF THE ASHES

Although I may not see it,
Beauty is everywhere.
Here in this pile of ashes,
My very life was spared.

When I chose temptation
Over all I know is right,
I started a mighty battle.
Thank God, Jesus won the fight.

When I feel I'm drowning—
A victim of my sins—
I turn my eyes to heaven
And invite him in.

He'll take that pile of ashes,
All the mess that I have made.
With all of my bad choices,
The price for them, he's paid.

I'll rise up from those ashes,
His Spirit inside me.
All the demons will be conquered,
And I will be set free.

As people look upon my life,
Knowing where I've been,
They'll know it must be Jesus.
Only beauty is now seen.

Jesus has transformed my life;
He's saved my very soul.
And now there's only beauty—
The beast has lost control.

I shall always thank my Savior
For all he's done for me.
He took my pile of ashes
And set me truly free.

REFLECTIONS

(What God's Spirit Said to Me)

LIGHT IN THE DARK

Life isn't always fair;
Things happen along the way.
Sometimes I just sit and stare;
There's nothing one can say.

I wonder why life's like that;
How could this happen to me?
I'm falling down an abyss—
Only darkness, no light to see.

God, help me; I can't make it.
Please get me out of here.
It's too much; I can't take it.
Help me through my fear.

And then I feel a gentle touch—
The hand of God above.
His comforting arms mean so much.
He tells me I am loved.

His love, it washes over me
And takes away my pain.
The peace he gives sets me free.
I'll live to soar again.

I'll rise up on wings of eagles;
My hope, it has returned.
My future's bright as it can be;
In the darkness, I have learned.

God is always with me,
Whatever life may bring.
I will always make it through
If I trust in him.

REFLECTIONS

(What God's Spirit Said to Me)

In All Things, Thanks

Thank you, God, for everything;
All things come from you.
All the blessings in my life,
Each time that you come through.

Thank you, God, for life itself—
Your special gift to me.
For every morning I awake,
Each day that I still breathe.

Thank you, God, for the people
You have placed in my life—
All my friends and family.
We're not torn apart by strife.

Thank you, God, for your creation;
It surrounds me everywhere.
I'm in awe of your majesty;
There's nothing to compare.

Thank you, God, for all you are:
Heavenly Father, the great I Am,
Holy Spirit, bringing peace and joy,
Jesus, Good Shepherd to your lambs.

Thank you, God, for your love;
You gave your Son for me
So that I could live with you
Now and eternally.

Reflections

(What God's Spirit Said to Me)

LETTING GO

In letting go there's freedom
From all that holds you down
And makes your life difficult,
So you can only frown.

Cast your cares on Jesus.
He's here to see you through,
To take away the pain and fear
And help with forgiveness, too.

When you let go and forgive,
That's where the blessings lie.
Jesus promises abundance
And fullness for your life.

But first you must forgive those
Who have done you any wrong.
Jesus has forgiven them,
And to him they all belong.

Jesus gave his life for them,
And he gave it up for you.
So you must forgive their sins;
It's the only thing to do.

To live a life of harmony
Filled with blessings and God's love,
Forgiveness is the only key.
It's an order from above.

When you let go and forgive
It's you who gets set free
From bitterness and anger.
Your life will be happy.

REFLECTIONS

(What God's Spirit Said to Me)

PURPOSE

Every day you're with me;
You'll never let me go.
No matter what each day brings,
You're here to help me grow.

You never will allow
More than I can bear.
I only have to trust you, Lord,
For I know you care.

You only want what's best for me.
You'll do whatever it takes
To love me and to bless my life.
It's always for my sake.

You made me in your image
To share my life with you,
So that you could bless me,
And I'd bless others, too.

To love you and to bless you
Is what you ask from me.
To love and live for others,
So in me, it's you they see.

You gave the ultimate sacrifice—
Your one and only Son.
He came and died just for me,
So we could live as one.

Then you sent your Spirit
To live in me each day,
To guide my each and every step
And help me find the way.

That's how much you love me.
I give each day to you;
Use it how you know is best.
Show me what to do.

REFLECTIONS

(What God's Spirit Said to Me)

SPIRALING

Spiraling, spiraling
Out of control.
Spiraling, spiraling,
Losing my soul.

Spiraling, spiraling
All the way down.
Spiraling, spiraling;
I've hit the ground.

How did it happen?
Where do I go?
There's dizzy confusion;
I feel so low.

Where can I turn?
Who can I trust?
Here on the ground
I taste only dust.

It's torture down here,
Not a friend to be found.
Someone, please help me
Turn my life back around.

God, are you real?
I've heard that you care.
Please help me; I've fallen.
I'm trapped in a snare.

I'm here at rock bottom
With no one to trust.
I've only got you;
Please help me, you must.

What can I give you?
A bargain I'll make.
What do you want
To get me out of this place?

I give you my life,
My heart, and my trust.
Now that you're with me,
The only way's up.

REFLECTIONS

(What God's Spirit Said to Me)

SUPERHERO

There is a superhero,
Who hung upon a tree
And gave his life long ago.
He is the great JC.

They thought that when they killed him
The dirty deed was done.
But when he died for my sins,
The battle was finally won.

With powers so amazing,
He rose from the dead
And saved us forever
With the blood that he'd shed.

He overcame the evil
That tried to bring him down.
His blood spilled out upon the cross
And drove the Devil out of town.

Whenever I'm in trouble,
He always comes around
And kicks that dirty villain
Right back underground.

He is an awesome hero—
The greatest of all time.
Because he gave his life for me,
Victory is mine.

This amazing superhero
Lives inside of me.
He overcame the villain
And set me truly free.

REFLECTIONS

(What God's Spirit Said to Me)

CUTS DEEP

Deep on the inside,
Hidden from view,
Is a pain unrelenting.
My life's all askew.

A wound underneath
Where no one can see:
A really deep cut
Inside of me.

On the outside there's nothing;
I seem to be fine.
But deep down I'm hurting
All of the time.

The pain won't let go;
It keeps tormenting me.
I must get it out
And set it free.

With a sense of compulsion,
Yet also control,
I cut on the outside
To let the pain go.

I cut at my skin
And feel some relief.
The pain on the inside
For a while is released.

But then it comes back
To hurt me again.
It's always there lurking.
Could the pain be my friend?

There's total confusion;
I can't work it out.
Why I like it, yet hate it.
What's this pain all about?

But here in my heart
There's a truth that I know:
Pain isn't my friend.
It's really my foe.

Living within me
Is my one true best friend.
He loves me completely,
And my heart he will mend.

He brings me comfort,
And he gives me peace.
He heals all the pain
Inside of me.

His presence is loving
And gentle and kind.
He'll heal all my wounds,
And my heart he will bind.

With him there is wholeness;
He's all that I need.
I surrender to him,
And the pain is set free.

REFLECTIONS

(What God's Spirit Said to Me)

Part of the Family

We are his special children,
Each and every one.
God forgave our sins long ago
When he sent his only Son.

Jesus came from heaven
And left his royal throne.
He dwelt here amongst us
And made this world his home.

He fully understands our ways
And all that brings us down.
He bore our sins for us
When he wore that thorny crown.

A holy, living sacrifice
So we could be set free,
Jesus gave his life for us
When he died upon the tree.

He didn't have to do it
But chose to die for us.
Now we can live in freedom
When in him we put our trust.

You see it didn't end there;
Jesus rose from the grave.
He overcame death for us
And is alive today.

We have a special purpose;
It's what he made us for—
To live our lives in unity.
His church should heed his call.

It's to go out into this world,
Amongst those who have been lost.
Let's speak of God's forgiveness
And what our salvation cost.

Jesus took away all our sins
And set us truly free.
That's how much he loves us;
He died for you and me.

REFLECTIONS

(What God's Spirit Said to Me)

SELF-IMAGE

When I look into the mirror
It makes me feel so bad.
I feel so fat and ugly,
And that makes me really sad.

I never see the beauty
Or who I truly am.
All I see is ugliness;
I've believed the Devil's scam.

I search and look around me;
There's beauty everywhere.
All the others look so awesome;
It's really so unfair.

I want to be more like them.
I've bought the Devil's lie
That I'm not good enough.
I must change; I've got to try.

So I purge my body.
I do whatever it takes
To make myself look beautiful,
And then I can feel great.

When I'm fit and skinny,
I'll be looking good.
And so I don't eat the food
That I know I should.

My body is my enemy;
It's what I must control,
But it's just so hard to do it.
This is eating at my soul.

God, help me, please, I'm falling
Into a deep, dark pit.
I know I can't keep doing this;
I must be rid of it.

This really bad self-image
Keeps tearing at my heart
And robbing me of my joy.
It rips my life apart.

I hear your kind, soft whisper
And feel your gentle, healing touch.
You've taken all my anguish
And filled me with your love.

You tell me how I'm beautiful—
Both inside and out.
Created in your image,
You've turned my life about.

God's made me just
the way he wants;
I'm perfect as I am.
He had my design in mind
And created me to a plan.

REFLECTIONS

(What God's Spirit Said to Me)

SPIDER'S WEB

The Enemy is a spider
Who tempts and lures you in.
He spins a web to catch you;
Then you're trapped in sin.

At first the web's enchanting;
You think that you'll be fine.
Beware; it's only a mirage
Made up of deceit and lies.

The web, it will ensnare you—
Body, mind, and soul.
Once you've entered into it,
The spider has control.

If only you'd have stayed away
And heeded the advice
Others tried to give you
On how the spider would entice.

But now the spider's got you,
And you don't know what to do.
The web is all around you;
There's no way to break through.

Although the trap had been set
So you wouldn't see,
The spider didn't count on
God's spirit in you and me.

It can never trap your spirit;
The spirit's much too strong.
So reach down deep inside you.
It's to God that you belong.

God's spirit will cut through the web
And set you free again.
He'll pick you up and
make things right;
On him you can depend.

So when a spider traps you
With his wily ways,
Remember, God's there with you;
Turn to him and pray.

REFLECTIONS

(What God's Spirit Said to Me)

CONFUSION SAYS

Confusion makes it difficult
To figure anything out.
Just when I think I know it all,
It turns my life about.

Confusion says, "It's much too hard;
You'll never make it through."
It leaves me in such turmoil,
Not knowing what to do.

Confusion whispers in my ear
And tries to make me doubt
Everything I do and say
And what my life's about.

Sometimes a loud, clanging noise
Here, inside my head.
It stops me from sleeping;
I toss and turn in bed.

Confusion tries to grip me
And says I won't succeed.
I need to take a hold of it
And drive it to its knees.

Confusion gets in the way
And tries to hold me back
From all I've been called to do.
It's a spiritual attack.

So when it rears its ugly head
And tries to cloud my mind,
I quiet my soul and trust in God.
His answers I will find.

I know that God will show the way
And guide my every step.
He'll steer my heart
the way he wants;
His destination's best.

REFLECTIONS

(What God's Spirit Said to Me)

"Enter" with Caution

The world, it has so many ways
Of trying to draw us in.
We must always be on our guard
And not give into sin.

The internet stands on neutral ground;
It conveys both bad and good.
We must choose to use it wisely
And do only what we should.

It's great to have the access
To all we want to know.
And when we put it to good use,
There are many seeds to sow.

But when it's used for evil,
It is the Devil's tool.
The internet's what we make of it.
Don't be the Devil's fool.

Make sure you only use it
For all that God intends.
It can be a useful weapon
When you chat with all your "friends."

So always pause; just stop and think
Before you hit the "Enter."
Is this something I should do,
Or could my choice be better?

REFLECTIONS

(What God's Spirit Said to Me)

BROKEN-HEARTED

Broken-hearted
Is how I feel.
Broken-hearted—
The pain, surreal.

Why'd you betray me?
I don't know.
The hurt goes deep.
Does it show?

I'm lonely and bruised,
All battered inside.
You've shattered my heart
And wounded my pride.

But I'll get through this;
I must move on.
The Spirit inside
Keeps me strong.

I face each day
And hold on to you,
Believing your Spirit
Will get me through.

You'll take my heart
That's been broken in two.
You'll bind it together
With your loving glue.

REFLECTIONS

(What God's Spirit Said to Me)

SALVATION'S CRY

God, help me to get over this;
I don't know what to do.
The problem's just too big for me;
I need you to get me through.

Help me, Lord; I need you.
Hold my hand today.
Bring me peace and comfort.
Send your love my way.

I feel so very desperate;
I'm hurting deep inside.
The pain's too much for me to bear,
No matter how I try.

I just can't find the answers;
I feel so very low.
I have no clue what I should do.
Please help me let this go.

Take this burden from me;
I need your peace today.
Show me that you love me.
Please save me, Lord, I pray.

REFLECTIONS

(What God's Spirit Said to Me)

"THE TEN"

There is a God who loves you
More than you'll ever know.
He only wants what's best for you,
So just stay in his flow.

A very long time ago
He came and helped us out
By writing a set of rules
On what life should be about.

So they'd be remembered,
He wrote them all in stone.
No one could ever change them;
These words were his very own.

The first few are about him
And the things he's done.
You must put him first in your life;
He is the holy one.

You are to worship only him—
No other things as well.
Use his name with respect,
Not when you want to yell.

He has his own special day
Set aside for him.
That's when you must stop and rest
And spend some time with him.

Your parents are important;
He made them just for you.
So always treat them nicely.
Respect them; he wants you to.

As for other people,
He loves them just like you.
So you must not try to harm them
With things you say or do.

Be faithful to your loved ones
And never cheat on them.
Don't be envious of
what others have.
On God you must depend.

The other two are simple:
Never steal or lie.
God's always right there with you;
He'll help you to get by.

These are the rules he gave to us.
But if you should fall short
Of doing all that he has asked,
Remember what he taught.

Because you're only human
You'll sometimes break his rules.
But your gracious God
still loves you.
Everything is cool.

If you're truly sorry
For what it is you've done,
God will forgive you
'Cause you're his special one.

REFLECTIONS

(What God's Spirit Said to Me)

DIVINE TOUCH

If your life has come undone,
You need to call on the one
Who can turn your world around.
Love and joy are to be found.

There is a power; it is divine,
And in Jesus, peace you'll find.
You only have to invite him in
And repent of your sin.

As I lay my hands on you
This awesome power is in you, too.
All you need to do is ask,
And God will help with every task.

You see, God loves you very much.
I've passed him on through my touch.
As I placed my hands on you
God came and lived in you, too.

Your life will never be the same
Because you now bear his name.
He set you apart; you belong to him.
He's taken away your every sin.

So just remember, he's always there
To help you with your every care.
His arms are always opened wide,
And in your heart he now resides.

REFLECTIONS

(What God's Spirit Said to Me)

My Vision

Where there is no vision, the people perish (Prov. 29:18 KJV).

Here is where you create a Vision Board for your life. To make a Vision Board you can use pictures or words or both. For more information on Vision Boards go to:

www.lillianworth.com

MY VISION

My Mission Statement

For more information on Purpose or Mission Statements go to:

www.lillianworth.com

The purpose of my life is to:

My mission is accomplished by/through/when I:

NOTES

Printed in the United States
By Bookmasters